# MYSTERIE
# RIGVEDA

## LOST TECHNOL(
## ENCODED IN THE EPICS

# Mysteries of the Rig Veda

HENRY ROMANO

Published by DTTV PUBLICATIONS, 2022.

MYSTERIES OF THE RIG VEDA

**First edition. August 20, 2022.**

Copyright © 2022 HENRY ROMANO.

ISBN: 978-1393290803

Written by HENRY ROMANO.

# Also by HENRY ROMANO

Myths and Legends of Japan
Myths and Legends of the Norse
The Ancient Mythologies of Peru and Mexico
Vedic Cosmology
Hindu Mythology and the Origins of Gods
Vedic Cosmos
Vedic Philosophy of the Kali Yuga
Sanskrit Mysteries of Vedic India
Ancient India and the Vedic Gods
The Secrets of Brahma
A History of Lost Knowledge in Sanskrit Literature
The Rise of Civilizations Concerning Vedic Knowledge
Decoding Hindu Chronology
Mysteries of the Rig Veda

Watch for more at https://www.dttvpublications.com/henryromano.

# Table of Contents

# HENRY ROMANO

To what extent is lost knowledge, advanced technology, and advanced philosophy encoded in the hymns of the Rigveda before we attempt to describe it? Is it possible to comprehend the true meaning of a book written in the remotest ages of Indian literature?

Identifying the appropriate method of interpretation for that ancient body of poetry is the key to answering this question. All ancient Indian texts contain old lost technology; take, for instance, the concept of the Vimana.

When the Rigveda first became known, scholars, as yet only familiar with the language and literature of classical Sanskrit, discovered that the Vedic hymns were composed in a mysterious ancient dialect and embodied an entirely different world of ideas than those they were familiar with.

India's Golden Age.

Hand-carved cave temples near Bellary in Southern India were vast and intricately carved from rock. Almost insurmountable difficulties hindered the interpretation of these hymns. A comprehensive commentary on the Rigveda exists that explains or paraphrases every word of its accolades. In the fourteenth century A.D., the great Vedic scholar Sayama lived in Vijayanagara ("City of Victory"), one of ancient India's most critical lost cities. His constant references to ancient authorities are believed to have preserved the Rigveda's true meaning in a traditional interpretation dating back thousands of years.

As a result, nothing further was necessary than explaining the original text, prevalent in India five centuries ago, as described in Sayama's work. The Rigveda has been translated by H. H., a professor of Sanskrit at Oxford, H. H. Wilson.

1

The late Professor Roth, who founded Vedic philology, took another line. In his view, Vedic interpretation should not be concerned with finding out what Sayama, or even Yska, who lived eighteen centuries earlier, ascribed to Vedic hymns, but instead with what the ancient poets themselves intended.

Rig Veda portrays sophisticated knowledge of time cycles, transportation, high technology, and advanced thinking and tools; however, following the commentators' comments cannot achieve such an end. Despite their valuable contributions to understanding later theological and ritual literature, with their familiar notions and practices, these last were not a continuous tradition from the time of the poets. They provided only the rules handed down from one interpreter to another, and they only began when the significance of the hymns was no longer fully understood.

It is important to remember that the Rig Veda is an oral tradition that requires interpretation. The interpretation could only occur when the hymns had become obscure; there could be no other tradition. Commentators preserved attempts to resolve difficulties while misinterpreting a vanished age's language and religious, mythological, and cosmic ideas according to their scholastic notions.

According to Yaska, there were some fundamental disagreements among older expositors and the different schools of interpretation that flourished before his time. According to him, there are seventeen predecessors whose explanations of the Veda are often conflicting. Nasatyau, an epithet of the Vedic Dioskouroi, is interpreted by one of them as "truthful, not false." One interpretation is "leaders of truth," while Yaska thinks it might mean "leaders of technology"!

In fact, one of Yska's predecessors, Kautsa, asserted that the science of Vedic exposition was useless because the Vedic hymns and formulas were obscure, insignificant, or contradictory. Only a tiny percentage of the hymns of the Rigveda are interpreted by Yaska himself. To explain what he tries to explain, he largely relies on etymological considerations.

He did not focus on lost knowledge and technology in the Rig Veda; he simply interpreted the hymns objectively. The same word is often used in more than one sense by him. Since he offers a variety of meanings, his renderings must be conjectural since there is no way to assume that the hymn's authors had more than one meaning in their minds.

There are times when Sayana departs from Yaska. With all the devices available, Yaska may have figured out the meaning of many words that scholars like Sayana, who lived nearly two thousand years later, could not. As a result, either the old interpreter was wrong, or the new one did not follow tradition. Sayana, independently of Yaska, gives many inconsistent explanations of a word, interpreting the same passage or commenting on different approaches. A defect of Sayana is that he limits his view, in most cases, to the one verse he has before him. Thus, he explains Canada, "autumn," as "fortified for a year," "new," and "belonging to Carad."

I also find Rig Veda's mathematics and numbers fascinating. What is the origin of Calculus? Calculus is credited to Newton in western textbooks. Arya Bhatta and Bhaskaracharya wrote Sanskrit mathematics texts many centuries before Newton, containing calculus. What is the origin of numbers? It was done by the Indians.

Sayana's commentary alone cannot provide a satisfactory translation of the Rigveda. Most material help can be derived from Sayana's interpretations, and he has been of the most excellent assistance in facilitating and speeding up the understanding of the Veda. His and Yaska's explanations of the Rigveda show that neither scholar had detailed information about many of the most challenging words, either from tradition or etymology. The authority of the commentators should not be taken as final unless it is supported by probability, context, or parallel passages in the hymns. It would be just as unreasonable to rely solely on the Talmud and Rabbis to understand the Hebrew books of the Old Testament.

Softwood trees are the only trees found in Europe. Ships made from those woods can sail the Mediterranean or smaller seas. Floating in the ocean is not ideal for them. When Vasco de Gama reached India, his vessels were on the verge of collapsing. To make that ship suitable for sea travel again, Indian marine engineers repaired it. Which country produces the most complicated wood? The Indian subcontinent. It is native to India and is referred to as Deva Tharu in Sanskrit. In addition to teak, mahogany and other hardwoods are native to India.With our knowledge of later Sanskrit, the other remains of ancient Indian literature, and our various philological instruments, we might have eventually discovered some information of value from Sayama.

As the first literary monument of the Indians, the Rigveda stands alone on an isolated mountain peak of remote antiquity. Roth rejected the commentators as our chief guides in understanding it. In terms of its strange and complex parts, it must therefore be interpreted primarily through itself; to use the words of an Indian commentator in another sense, it must be self-demonstrating and shine by its light. The Rigveda can also be better understood by a qualified European than by a Brahman interpreter, according to Roth. With the historical faculty and a broader intellectual horizon, he has an unfettered judgment unaffected by theological bias.

Therefore, Roth sought to analyze all parallel passages, considering context, grammar, and etymology, while consulting, though perhaps with insufficient attention, the traditional interpretations. In this way, he analyzed the Rigveda historically within the context of Sanskrit. In addition, he sought assistance from outside by using the comparative method, relying on the Avesta, which is so closely related to the Rigveda in language and matter, as well as the results of comparative philology, resources unknown to traditional scholars.

Ships with 100 oars are mentioned in the Rig Veda. Those ships returned to India after sailing across seven oceans. During pre-Christian times, Greek and Roman visitors to India wrote that the Brahmins knew the earth was a globe and could reach the same place after sailing through the seven oceans. Buddhist Jataka stories describe large Indian ships carrying seven hundred people. The Artha Sastra represents the Board of Shipping and the Commissioner of Port, who supervise sea traffic.

Considering the short time and the small number of laborers, only two or three of whom are native to this country, the progress already made in solving many fundamental problems presented by Vedic literature has been surprising. Between 1852 and 1875, Roth and Bohtlingk published the great Sanskrit Dictionary in seven volumes, which laid the foundation for the scientific interpretation of the Vedas. It is now accepted by every scientific student of Veda that Roth's method is correct. In the present day, however, native tradition is more fully exploited than Roth himself was able to do, for it has become apparent that extant Indian scholarship should not be overlooked.

During the period of Vaivasvata, the first geographical survey of the world took place. At that time, maps were used to demarcate agricultural lands, towns, and villages. An accurate world map drawn on a flat surface with a precise scale is described in detail in the Brahmanda Purana. In Surya Siddhanta, the earth is represented by a wooden globe with horizontal circles, equatorial circles, and further divisions. According to the Padma Purana, world maps were prepared and maintained in book form and with care and safety.

This has resulted in a greater understanding of Indian antiquity than was previously possible through native misinterpretations. Future generations of scholars will need to do much more, especially in a detailed and minute investigation, because Vedic research is only the product of the last fifty years and, despite the labors of many Hebrew scholars over the centuries, many passages remain obscure or disputed in the Psalms and Revelation Books of the Old Testament. The modern scholarship that has already deciphered the cuneiform writings of Persia and the rock inscriptions of India and discovered the languages hidden under these mysterious characters will solve many insoluble problems today.

"Wootz" steel is mentioned in the Rig Veda. There is evidence that steel was manufactured in South India during ancient times. Indian steel ingots were sold to Europe by the Arabians for a profit. Scientist Benjamin Huntsman was sent to India by the queen of Britain in 1746 to discover the secret of making steel. A report was submitted to the queen by Huntsman after he spent years in India. According to historical records, he started his foundry in his hometown without writing a vital secret. Because Henry Bessemer's process of making steel was essentially an Indian crucible, it is unnecessary to describe how the secret reached him. In Europe, casting was another contribution made by Indians. During that time, wood was used for the frames of machine tools. As early as the 1300s, Britain had mechanical devices like clocks. Not produced by precision machines but by skilled craftspeople. To manufacture the high-precision machine tools, the structural components of the machine tools had to be cast using Indian casting methods, and their other members had to be made using Indian steel-making methods. During the 1800s, this was a vital component of the so-called Industrial Revolution in Europe.

We now have access to Vedic thought through the golden key of scholarship. There are only ten books in Rigveda that contain secular poetry; most of the poems are religious lyrics. Vedic hymns praise the gods' greatness and beneficence and ask for cattle, children, prosperity, long life, and victory from them. Most hymns in the Vedic pantheon are addressed to the gods. According to Sanskrit scholars, a collection of primitive popular poetry is not what the Rigveda is. It is instead a body of skilfully composed hymns, prepared by a priestly class and meant to accompany the Soma offering and the fire offering of melted butter, both of which were offered by a ritual that was not as straightforward as once believed. However, it was undoubtedly more superficial than the elaborate system of the Brahmana period. Its poetry is marred by frequent references to the offering, especially in praise of Agni and Soma, two great ritual deities. Aeronautics was the subject of many ancient Sanskrit texts in India. A few of them are Yantra Sarvaswa, Vimaana Chandrika, Vyoma Yaana Tantra, and Vyoma Yaanarka of Dandi Natha. There were topics such as Maargadhi Karana (Navigation and control of speed during flight), Lohaadhi Karana (alloys used for aircraft components), and Saktyaadhi Karana (multiple fuels used in aircraft production). In Para Sabda Grahakata, flight tracks, navigation systems, and pilots' conversations are monitored. According to Maharshi Gotham, only one model, Pushpaka Vimaanam, became popular in the Ramayana.

A solar-powered engine is used in Tripura Vimaanam to travel on land, underwater, and in the air, according to the Vaimaanika Sastra. Space shuttles are a cross between aircraft and rockets called Sakuna Vimaanam. During the British rule in India, the British stole most of our Sanskrit manuscripts. A 1500-foot-high plane was constructed in 1895 by Sivasankar Thalpad of Bombay. He taught Vedic studies at the J.J. College of Arts. A few rare Sanskrit manuscripts provided him with the technology. Praacheena Vimaana Vidye Chaasodha is another book he wrote in Marathi. It was witnessed by many people, including Maharaja of Baroda Lalaji Rayanji. In the wake of Prof. Thalapad's untimely death, his legal heirs sold all his scripts and materials to the British.

In these conditions, it is much more natural than one might expect. A Rig Veda god is almost always a personification of a natural phenomenon, which explains its beautiful and noble imagery. Hymns are straightforward and unaffected in their diction. The frequency and length of words in classical Sanskrit contrast with the sparing use of compound words. Besides the tributes to the ritual deities, where it gets entangled in conceit and mystical obscurity, the thought is usually artless and direct. Because of the minimal nature of the theme in these cases, the priestly singers must have been forced to strive for variety by using enigmatical phrases to express the same idea.

In one of the Brahmanas, the saying that the gods love the recondite tells us already that the early period was also fond of subtlety and challenging modes of expression. It is also evident in some hymns that Sanskrit poets played with words to inordinate lengths. Literary merit is evident in the hymns of the Rigveda, as is to be expected from many centuries of poets. Many poems display a high degree of poetic excellence, while others contain commonplace and mechanical language. Considering that we have the oldest poetry of the Rig Veda, the composition skill is remarkably high.

The closing stanza often refers to the need for these early seers' art to produce an excellent hymn for the gods. An artisan's deftly crafted car is often compared to the poet's work. Rishis liken their prayers to delicate and well-woven garments, while another compares their praise songs to brides for their lovers. A poet praises the gods based on their knowledge and ability, and they express their feelings. Rigvedic poets know everything about the metallurgy of the later doctrine of revelation, regardless of which gods granted seers the gift of song.

There is proof of this in the iron pillar in Delhi, which does not rust even today. There are many other ones of this kind in India; many others exist. Powder metallurgy technology has been confirmed by the Russians who took scrapings from the pillar. Using powder metallurgy, the so-called space-age technology of today can only produce small pieces; these are used as cutting tool tips. Using powder metallurgy, how could our ancients make such a large pillar? The post has a challenge - it is like a time capsule. Are we capable of surpassing the achievements of our ancient ancestors?

Vedic hymns are monotonous, as is often said. In each book, the melodies create the impression that the same deity is frequently grouped together. Nearly five hundred hymns in the Rigveda address two gods alone, so, surprisingly, there are so many variations on the same theme.

Our understanding is that the hymns of the Rigveda are mainly invocations of the gods; their content is mythological. Unlike any other literature, this mythology represents an earlier thought stage. This is a sufficiently primitive artifact to make it possible to see how natural phenomena became gods through personification. In his ordinary life, the Vedic Indian has never observed action or movement not caused by an agent acting or moving, so he still refers to such events as personal agents, which are inherent in the phenomena. In awe of nature, he still observes its workings.

A poet wonders why the Sun does not fall from the sky; another splendor where the stars go by day; and third marvels that all rivers never fill the ocean. The unchanging regularity of the Sun and Moon and the unwavering recurrence of Dawn suggested that nature has a regular order. We find in the Rigveda that the concept of this general law, called ita (properly "the course of things"), is first applied to the fixed rules of offering (right) and then to those of morality (directly).

The light was not used as a measure of length by our ancient seers. A massive mass bends light if it passes near it. Einstein discovered this. Can you call something "which bends" unchangeable? Over time, everything created changes; there is no such thing as a universal constant. In addition, light's velocity does not deviate from this law. A star's stored energy determines the rate of light. Krita Yuga had a higher speed of light than today, even if only by a small fraction. In addition, modern science acknowledges that the Sun has lost much of its power over billions of years.

If other stars in the universe emit light faster than the Sun and have greater stored energies, then they must have more excellent accumulated points than the Sun. Yes, of course. After modern science develops more sophisticated equipment than it currently has, this will be confirmed. What prevents us from using our ancient knowledge? A law of nature says everything in creation must go through cycles of time. Sleep must follow a period of wakefulness, and light must follow a period of darkness.

Additionally, the human mind will not give due value to satisfaction without a period of sorrow following a period of happiness. A period of sadness will lead to a period of joy that is much more heartwarming. The higher psyche of Indians is now at rest as a result of that law. Are you expecting it to awaken soon? Is it possible to see it during our lifetime? That's right. India is predicted to regain some of its prestigious glory in about two decades by some Indian and Western astrologers. The Rigveda presents a relatively primitive mythological phase but contains several inherited concepts from previous eras. In the Avesta, several Vedic deities are paralleled with those of the Persian and Indian ancestors. There are several notable examples, such as Yama, the God of the dead, identical with Yima, ruler of paradise, and especially Mitra, whose Persian counterpart, Mithra, achieved worldwide diffusion in the Roman Empire and came closer to monotheism than any other paganism.

———◉———

THE CULT OF THE HERB Soma (the Avestan Haoma) and the worship of fire can also be traced back to that early age. Cows were also venerated at that time. There must have been religious hymn poetry even then, for the Avesta and the Rigveda agree on stanzas of four eleven-syllable lines (trishUbh and Gayatri), and there also seem to be a few lines of eight syllables (anushUbh and sauyA2).

In addition to Heaven and earth as primeval, universal parents, many magical beliefs are probably derived from antiquity. As far back as the Indo-European period, the concept of "god" (deva-s, Lat. deu-s) and heavenly father as a divine father (Dyau pit, Gr. Zeus parent, Lat. Jupiter) had been in use. According to the Rigveda poets, there are three domains in the universe: earth, air, and Heaven. This division may have also been known to the ancient Greeks. The Rigveda mentions this famous triad constantly, either directly or indirectly. Lightning, rain, and wind are air phenomena, while solar phenomena are called Heaven. While they are supposed to dwell only in the third world, the world of light, the various gods conduct their actions throughout the three worlds. In mythology, the air is often referred to as a sea, the dwelling place of the celestial waters, while massive rainless clouds are sometimes portrayed as rocks or mountains or as the castles of demons who fight the gods. Thundering rain clouds become cows whose milk gives fatness to the earth as they shed milk.

Sun, Dawn, Fire, and Wind are almost exclusively personified natural phenomena in Rigveda. Most gods are more or less connected to their physical foundations, except for a few deities from an older period. Personifications, therefore, lack a definite outline and a sense of individuality. In addition, the phenomena behind the personifications share some characteristics with other wonders of the same domain but have few distinctive features. The attributes of Dawn, Sun, and Fire are luminous, dispelling darkness, and appearing in the morning.

As a result, each God has a few essential qualities, combined with many other standard, such as brilliance, power, beneficence, and wisdom. The common attributes in prayer and praise hymns tend to obscure the distinctive ones. A god from different departments of nature with striking similarities is likely to become more like another. Invoking deities in pairs is a particular Vedic practice that encourages assimilation. In such combinations, the attributes of one God are transferred to the other, even when the latter appears alone.

Almost every power can be attributed to a deity, making identification straightforward. Thus, when the Fire-god, summoned by himself, is called a slayer of the demon Vṛitra, he receives an attribute distinct from the thunder-god Indra, with whom he is usually associated. This type of title frequently appears in Rigveda. A poet addressing the fire god explains: "At your birth, O Agni, you are Varu'a; when kindled, you are Mitra; to the worshipper, you are Indra."

Moreover, mystical speculations on Agni, so important a god in the eyes of a priesthood devoted to a fire cult, on his many appearances as separate fires on earth, and on Various gods are merely different manifestations of one divine being since Vedic poets often refer to them in riddles as atmospheric fires in lightning and celestial fires in the Sun. Over one passage of the Rigveda contains this idea. Thus, the author of a recent hymn (164) of the first book says: "The one being priests speak of; they call it Agni, Yama, Mataricvan." In the last book, a seer notes that priests and poets have made the bird (the Sun) into many through words. This shows how polytheism had taken on a monotheistic tinge by the end of the Rigvedic period.

Sometimes you are shadowed by the pantheistic idea of a deity who represents all the gods and nature. In a cosmogonic hymn, the Creator is described as the one God who overrules all gods and as the one God who embraces all things. The Hindu Vedanta philosophy is still the most popular system of thought today because it developed from this germ of pantheism in later Vedic literature.

Even in the oldest parts of the Rigveda, the poets invoked different gods as if each were paramount, giving rise to Professor Max Müller's theory of Henotheism or Kathenotheism, according to which the seers believed in individual gods. He alternately regarded the God addressed as the highest and treated him as if he were a separate and chief deity, all by himself. However, the exaggeration found in the Rigveda has little to do with anything more than how a singer would instinctively magnify the particular God he is invoked with. Almost every pantheon member found a place in the Soma ritual, which the Rishis knew in detail.

According to Vedic poets, they are described as the offspring of Heaven and Earth, or sometimes of other gods. Several passages also mention earlier gods, implying different generations. However, there is no evidence that the poets thought Indra and other gods were immortal. Neither were the gods considered immortal initially since immortality is said to have been conferred on them by specific deities, such as Agni and Savitri, or gained by drinking Soma. There was only a cosmic age in the post-Vedic view.

A Vedic god's physical appearance is anthropomorphic. Thus, the human head, face, eyes, arms, hands, feet, and other body parts are attributed to them. The forms of these creatures are shadowy, and their parts or limbs are sometimes referred to figuratively. As a result, the tongue and limbs of the fire god represent his flames; the arms of the sun-God represent his rays, and his eye only symbolizes its orb. Since the external shape of the gods was vaguely conceived, while their connection with natural phenomena was usually still apparent, it is easy to understand why no reference is made in the Rigveda to images of the gods, still, less of temples, which implies the existence the first to mention idols.

Agni conveys the offering to the gods in Heaven through their vehicles. The gods often appear as warriors armed with spears, battleaxes, bows, and arrows, wearing coats of mail and helmets. The horses, kine, goats, and deer they ride on drive luminous cars through the air. They are viewed as living in harmony; only the overbearing and warlike Indra brings discord.

Vedic Indians were often regarded as beneficent beings, bestowing long lives and prosperity on them. There are no injurious features in any other deity but Rudra. A lesser evil, such as disease, originates with minor demons, whereas a greater evil, such as drought and darkness, originates with powerful monsters such as Vritra. It brings out the beneficent spirit of the gods even more strikingly when these demons are defeated.

There is also a sacred aspect to the Vedic gods. The truthful and the upright are their friends and guardians. A civilization's ethical standards are only reflected in di morality. Thus, even the connection of

Varuna, the most moral of the gods, with justice is not to prevent him from applying craft against the hostile and the deceitful man. Moral elevation is a less prominent characteristic of the gods than greatness and power.

In Rigveda, the relationship between worshippers and gods depends on worshippers' will, prayers, and offerings. However, the expectation of something in return for the offering is frequently apparent, as the keynote of many hymns is, "I give to thee that you may give to me." It is also often stated that hymns, offerings, and especially offerings of Soma produce the gods' might and valor. Vedic pretensions can be found here, which have been accumulating since the Vedic era.

In the White Yajurveda, it is stated that a Brahman with correct knowledge has control over the gods. As the Brahmanas say, there are two kinds of gods, Devas, and Brahmans, the latter of whom are held as deities. Similarly, the Brahmanas portray the offering as all-powerful, able to control not only the gods but nature itself.

Several times the Rigveda expresses the number of gods as thrice eleven, corresponding to each division of the threefold universe. Occasionally, other gods are also mentioned in addition to the thirty-three gods mentioned above. Various groups, such as storm-gods, cannot be included in this number.

Nevertheless, few deities in the Rigveda are significant enough to receive at least three entire hymns. At least 250 psalms are dedicated to Indra, the thunder god, Agni with over 200, and Soma with more than 100, while only three each are devoted to Parjanya, the rain god, and Yama, the dead God. These two extremes are followed by a wide range of positions between them. Three thousand years ago, the two great deities of modern Hinduism, Vishnu, and Rudra (the early form of Civa), should have been equally important, though far below the chief deities in the Rigveda. In general, they stand out as being extraordinarily benevolent and terrible.

Personifying the sky as a god never progressed beyond a primitive stage in Rigveda, being almost entirely limited to the concept of paternity. Dyaus (the Greek Zeus) is one of the oldest gods of Heaven. Six hymns celebrate Dyaus and Prithivi as universal parents. A few passages mention Dyaus as a bull, ruddy and bellowing downwards, referring to the fertilizing power of rain and lightning and thunder. Moreover, he is once likened to a black steed adorned with pearls, an allusion to the nocturnal starry sky. This God is described as being equipped with a bolt by one poet and smiling through the clouds by another. A smile is frequently compared with dazzling white objects in classical Sanskrit, just as the verb "to smile" (smi) alludes to lightning in other passages of the Rigveda.

There is no way to know what natural phenomenon lies behind Varuna's personification since it has developed so far that it can only be deduced from his character traits. His name does not at the same time refer to a natural phenomenon, like that of Dyaus, which may explain his not being a creation of Indian mythology but from an older heritage. Varuna-s means "encompassing sky," and maybe it's the same as the Greek Ouranos, although the phonetic identification, while challenging, can be made.

Despite being invoked in fewer hymns than Indra, Agni, or Soma, Varuna stands as the greatest of the Vedic gods alongside Indra. Conversely, Varuna is the great upholder of physical and moral order (Rita). Hymns addressed to him are more devout and ethical than any others. In their character, they are often similar to the Hebrew psalms, the most exalted portion of the Veda. The tranquil sway of Varuna is explained by his association with the regularly recurring celestial phenomena, the course of the heavenly bodies seen in the sky; Indra's combative and sometimes capricious nature is explained by the variable and uncertain strife of the elements in the thunderstorm.

Using the Vedic poets' words, one can sketch the character and power of Varuna as closely as possible. Varuna's law separates Heaven and earth. The golden swing (the Sun) shined in Heaven because of him. The Sun now has a wide path to follow. It is Varuna's breath that reverberates through the air. As a result of his ordinances, the moon shines brightly at night, and the stars are evident at night but not during the day. By his decree, he makes the rivers flow. Because of his occult power, the rivers swiftly flowing into the ocean are not filled with water.

Clouds cover the mountains as he pours the water from the inverted cask on the ground, moistening it. Aerial waters are his primary connection; seas are rarely.There is a lot of discussion about Varuna's omniscience. He knows how birds fly in the sky, how ships navigate oceans, and how far-traveling winds travel. He knows everything that has been done or will be done in secret. The truth and falsehood of men are witnessed by him. No creature can wink without him. As a moral governor, Varuna is unparalleled. Those who violate his ordinances, which he castigates, arouse his wrath. Often, he is described as binding sinners with fetters. Falsehood is repelled, hated, and punished by him, but he is gracious to the penitent. In addition to forgiving men for their sins, he forgives their fathers' sins. A suppliant who regularly transgresses his laws is spared, and a person who has broken his ordinances out of thoughtlessness is gracious. Unlike other deities, Varuna has no hymns without the prayer for worldly goods, just as other gods have hymns about forgiveness of guilt.

Only the dominion of waters, a small part of Varuna's original sphere, remained as the Creator, Prajapati, became a chief deity. He is only an Indian Neptune, God of the sea, based on the Atharva-Veda and post-Vedic mythology.

The Rigveda represents the Sun's activity through five solar deities. In ancient times, Mitra, the "Friend," was envisioned as the beneficent side of the Sun's power. Since the Indo-Iranian period, his individuality has almost entirely been lost in Rigveda, practically merging with

Varuna's. Only one hymn addresses him alone, while he is constantly invoked with the former.

Surya (cognate to the Greek Helios) is one of the most concrete solar deities. Despite being named after the luminary, he never loses sight of his connection to it. Dawn is said to bring the vision of the gods, and Surya's eye is often mentioned. Being all-seeing, he observes all creatures and mortals' good and bad deeds. Those who move and are fixed are protected by him. As a result of Surya's awakening, men do their work and pursue their objectives. It is described that he rides a car drawn by seven steeds.

The stars slink away like thieves as Surya rolls into the darkness. In the lap of the dawns, he shines forth. In addition to being called the husband of Dawn, he is also referred to as her husband. He was placed in Heaven by the gods as a form of Agni. As he traverses space, he is often compared to a bird or eagle. To prolong life, he measures the days. Disease and evil dreams are driven away by him. He is prayed to proclaim men sinless to Mitra and Varuna at his rising. "All-creating" means he is responsible for the creation of all entities.

Savitri, who represents the Sun's quickening activity, is also addressed with eleven hymns, or about the same number as Surya. He is predominately a golden deity with golden hands and arms and a golden car. He extends his strong golden arms to the ends of the earth, blessing and arousing all beings. As he drives his golden car, he sees all creatures moving downwards and upwards. Dawn shines after him. With yellow-haired Savitri, the Sun's rays continue to brighten the east. By driving away demons and sorcerers, he removes evil dreams. Gods receive immortality, and men live a long time. In addition, he leads departed spirits to the dwelling places of the righteous. Despite the power of Indra and Varua, no god could resist Savitri's independent sway and will. Venus, the evening star, is frequently associated with Savitri.

TRADITIONALLY, GOD is invoked as the Stimulator at the beginning of Vedic study with the most famous Rigvedic stanza, which every orthodox Hindu still repeats in morning rituals. Due to the meter, it is also known as "the Gayatri" due to the name of the goddess:

An anthology of modern poetry would likely produce a similar effect if twenty or thirty lyrics were read. Among the peculiarities of the hymns to Savitri is the repeated play on the root su ("to stimulate") from which it is derived.

The Rigveda invokes Pushan in eight hymns. "Prosperity" is his name, and his character is based on the beneficent power of the Sun manifested primarily as a pastoral deity. He carries a goad, and goats draw his car. With his goad, he teaches cattle and protects roads. He gives welfare as he protects men and cattle on earth and guides mortals to the abodes of bliss in the next world. The dead are guided on the far path to the father because he knows Heaven's ways.

The Rigveda lists Vishnu as the fourth most frequently invoked deity, less regularly than Surya, Savitri, and Pushan, but historically he is the most important. He is considered one of the greatest among the two principal gods of Hinduism. He takes three strides, which may represent the Sun's course through the universe's three divisions. Heaven is his highest step, where the gods and the fathers live. In his longing for this abode, the poet writes:

It is my wish to reach that, his well-loved dwelling,

Blessed are those who devote themselves to the gods:

He is our relative in Vish*u's highest step,

The Spring of nectar is at the end of mighty strides.

Originally, Vishnu was conceived as the Sun, not in his general character, but as a swiftly moving luminary traversing the three worlds. The three steps he took are said to be for the benefit of humanity in several passages.

The Brahmanas relate a myth about Vishnu appearing as a dwarf as an artifice to reclaim the earth that has been possessed by demons.

Avatars ("descents to earth") or avatars, which he adopted for the good of humanity, developed in post-Vedic mythology.

In almost all hymns, Ushas, the goddess of Dawn, is addressed, and she is invoked most frequently. There are, however, more than twenty hymns dedicated to her. "Shining One" is cognate with the Latin Aurora and Greek Eos. Dawn is never far from the poet's mind when addressing the goddess.

The adoration with which the thoughts of these priestly singers turned to her alone among the goddesses, even though she received no share in the offering of Soma like the other gods, seems to indicate that the glories of the Dawn, more splendid than those we are accustomed to seeing in Northern India, deeply impressed the minds of these early poets. Among all the descriptions of religious poetry, she is the most graceful creation, unsurpassed in its charm. Neither priestly subtleties nor allusions to the offering mar the natural beauty of the imagery here.

Here are some of the utterances about the Dawn goddess, culled from various hymns, expressed as closely as possible in the words of their composers to enable the reader to assess the merit of this poetry. As the daughter of Dyaus, Ushas is a radiant maiden born in the sky. She is the brighter sister of Night. She glows with the light of her lover, Surya, a young man, a girl. Her carriage rides on ruddy steeds or kine, drawn by splendid horses.

Her bosom is exposed as she wears gay attire like a dancer. In the east, a maiden clothed in light appears to reveal her charms. After a bath, she emerges resplendent. Her light does not withhold its light from small or significant things. As the cows (issue from) their stalls, she opens the gates of Heaven wide. She appears to be herding cattle with her radiant beams. Her black robe of Night is removed, warding off evil spirits and the hated darkness. Birds fly up when she awakens them with her feet: she is the breath and life of all life.

Ushas shines, causing birds to fly up from their nests and men to seek nourishment. She leads the charm of pleasant voices with her radiant movements of sweet sounds. Each day, she appears at the appointed place, never infringing on order and the gods; she follows the order path, never losing her direction. Having shone in former days, she will continue to shine in the future, never aging, immortal.

In contrast to the eternal recurrence of the Dawn, the solitude and stillness of the early morning sometimes suggested pensive thoughts about human life's fleeting nature.

Celestial light deities include the twin morning gods Acvins, who are most often invoked. They are eternally young and handsome, appearing in the early Dawn when the darkness still stands among the ruddy cows. The sun-maiden Surya rides with them in a car. Its parts are all golden, and it is bright and sunlike. At the yoking of their vehicle, Ushas is born.

The Acvins are depicted as succoring divinities in many myths. A ship or ship is used to rescue people from distress, especially from the ocean. The blind get sight, and the lame walk through them. They are divine physicians. Vicpala, whose leg was cut off in some conflict, was once provided with an iron limb by the Acvins after her leg was amputated. As sons of Zeus and brothers of Helen, the Dioskouroi share many characteristics with the two famous horse riders of Greek mythology. In terms of origin, the twilight, half-dark, half-light, or morning and evening stars appear to be the most likely candidates.

Air is ruled by Indra, the deity of air. Among the Vedic Indians, he is their favorite God and national deity. He is sufficiently praised in the Rigveda, as over one-fourth of it is devoted to his praise. As a legacy of being handed down from a bygone age, Indra has become more humanoid and surrounded by mythological imagery than any other Vedic god. His character is sufficiently significant. His mythical essence is formed by the conquest of the demon of drought or darkness named Vritra, the "Obstructor," and the consequent liberation of the waters or the winning of light.

There is an ever-recurring theme in this myth for the Rishis. When Indra strikes Vritra like a tree with his bolt, Heaven and earth tremble. A thunderbolt in hand, exhilarated by copious drinks of Soma and escorted by the Maruts, Indra enters the fray. There is a terrible conflict going on. The combat is described as being repeated constantly by him. As a result, the myth is based on a perpetual renewal of natural phenomena. When describing Indra's exploits, poets rarely mention the physical elements in the thunderstorm. He seldom sheds rain, but rivers and pent-up waters are constantly released.

Various names are given to clouds, including cow, udder, Spring, cask, or pale. Lighting is the "bolt," and thunder is cows' lowings or dragons' roars. Moreover, they are rocks (Adri), encompassing the cows that Indra released. Indra casts down demons from these mountains. Thus, they often become fortresses (purs) of the demons, which are ninety, ninety-nine, or a hundred in number, and are described as "moving," "autumnal," or "made of stone or iron." As a result of the significance of the Vritra myth, Indra's chief and the particular epithet is Vritrahan, meaning "slayer of Vritra." Indra slew Vritra broke the castles, made a channel for the rivers, pierced the mountain, and gave the cows to his friends in one stanza.

Light and the Sun are won through the liberation of the waters. During conflicts with earthly enemies, Indra is invoked more frequently than any other deity as a helper. When Indra slayed the dragon Vritra with his bolt, releasing the waters for man, he placed the Sun in the heavens, or the Sun shone forth when Indra blew the dragon from the sky. While evaluating Indra's excesses, it is essential to remember that the exhilaration of Soma had a religious significance in the eyes of the Vedic poets. The occasional immoral traits in Indra's character account for the more advanced anthropomorphism of his nature.

He sometimes commits acts of capricious violence, such as killing his father or destroying Dawn's car. He is especially addicted to Soma, which he consumes in enormous quantities to perform his warlike feats. Indra boasts of his greatness and power in one entire hymn, intoxicated with Soma. The piece is of little poetic merit, but it is fascinating as the earliest literary description of the mental effects of intoxication, braggadocio.

The Avesta describes Indra as a demon. The Vedic epithet Vritrahan also appears there as verethraghna, the name of the God of victory. Accordingly, in the Indo-Iranian period, a god probably resembled Vritra-slaying, victorious Indra.

Varuna was more important in the Indo-Iranian period of the Rigveda than Indra, who became inferior to him later in Vedic history. Their importance was about equality in the earlier period of Rigveda. Despite being subordinate to Brahma-Vishnu-Civa, Indra became the Brahmanas and Epics chief of the Indian Heaven.

Lightning is associated with at least three lesser air deities. Among them is the somewhat obscure God Trita, who is only mentioned in detached verses of the Rigveda. The Avesta refers to this God as an Indo-Iranian God. Lightning is the "third" (Greek, tritos). Aptya, his frequent epithet, appears to mean "watery."

Due to his resemblance to Indra, he was gradually ousted. Apam napat, the "Son of Waters," is another rare deity from the Rigveda, dating from the Indo-Iranian era. He is depicted as clothed in lightning and shining in the water without fuel. Thus, there is no doubt that he represents lightning produced by rain clouds. A divine being, Mataricvan, rarely mentioned in the Rigveda, is described as having brought down fire from Heaven, like Prometheus in Greek mythology. He most likely represents a celestial form of Agni, God of fire, with whom he is sometimes identified. Later Vedas, Brahmanas, and subsequent literature simply refer to wind by this name.

In Rigveda, Rudra has a different position than his historical successor at a later age. His name is mentioned less frequently than Vish*u, but he is celebrated in three or four hymns. He usually uses a bow and arrows, but lightning shafts and thunderbolts are occasionally assigned. The hymns dedicated to him express fear of his terrible beams and deprecation of his Wrath. He is described as fierce, like a wild beast. Later Vedic literature still emphasizes his malevolence.

As a demon, Rudra isn't purely malevolent. Man and beast are beseeched for protection from calamity, blessings, and welfare. In addition to being lauded as the most excellent physician, he is often mentioned for his healing powers. After the Vedic period, the euphemistic epithet civa, which means "auspicious," became his familiar name, though not only in the younger Vedas.

In the Rigveda, the Maruts, or Storm-gods, form a group thrice seven or sixty. They are the sons of Rudra and Price, the mottled cloud-cow. In ancient times, they were compared with fires at birth and called "born from lightning's laughter."

They are a group of young warriors armed with spears or battle-axes and wearing helmets. Mostly armlets and anklets, they are adorned with golden ornaments.

Showers cover the Sun's eye, and they wear rain robes. They shed the rain as a primary function. Milk is poured on the earth; fat (ghee) is shed; thundering springs are milked; mead is run on the ground; the heavenly pot is poured out.

Indra calls the Maruts singers about the sound of the winds. All of his celestial conflicts are fought with them. Vayu, or Vata, is not a prominent deity in the Rigveda, with only three hymns dedicated to him. Indra is the main personification of Vayu, while Parjanya is the only anthropomorphic rain god associated with Vata. As fast as thought, Vayu has a roaring velocity. A team or a pair of ruddy horses pull his shining car. His companion is Indra, who sits in this car with a golden seat and touches the sky. Wind, also known as Vata, is celebrated more concretely. Va, derived from his name, means "to blow." In his house, he keeps a treasure that extends life and heals.

The Rigveda mentions Parjanya only thirty times and invokes him in only three hymns. In several passages, the name still simply means "raincloud." Thus, personification is always closely associated with the rainstorm, where the rain cloud becomes an udder, a pail, or a water skin. It is often said that Parjanya sheds rain like a bull.

Four hymns in the Rigveda praise the Waters as goddesses. Personification doesn't go much further than depicting them as mothers, young wives, and goddesses who offer boons. As daughters, they produce Agni, whose lightning form is Apam Napat, or "Son of Waters." The holy waters cleanse from moral guilt, violence, cursing, and lying sins and are invoked to remove defilement. Long life, healing, and immortality are all provided by them. In the waters, Soma delights in lovely maidens. He approaches them as lovers; they bow down to him.

The Rigveda personifies and invokes several rivers as deities. The Sindhu or Indus is celebrated in one hymn, while Vipac and Cutudri are praised in another. Three entire hymns and many detached verses are devoted to Sarasvati, the river goddess. In some streams, the goddess is personified much more extensively, but the poets never lose sight of the river's connection to her. Mothers, rivers, and goddesses cannot compare to her. Wealth, plenty, nourishment, and offspring flow from her unfailing breast. Poets pray that their love will not be snatched away from them by strangers.

The river goddess in Rigveda is identified with Vach, goddess of speech, and became the goddess of eloquence and wisdom in post-Vedic mythology, invoked as a muse and regarded as Brahma's wife. From the great mountain, she is called to descend from the sky. Those expressions may have suggested the celestial origin and descent of the Ganges, which is familiar to post-Vedic mythology.

Among the terrestrial deities, Agni is the most important. Over 200 hymns are dedicated to him, making him the most prominent Vedic God after Indra. In the Veda, ritual poetry revolves around the personification of the sacrificial fire, the center of which captivates the attention of the Rishis. Agni is also a common name for the element (Latin, igni-s); the deity is not anthropomorphic. God's bodily parts are clearly connected to the phenomena of terrestrial fire, mainly in its sacrificial nature. Having a butter-backed, butter-faced, or butter-haired appearance, Agni is also flame-haired and has a tawny beard, alluding to the oblation of ghee.

Sharp, shining, golden, or iron teeth and scorching jaws are characteristic of him. A sharp tooth allows him to eat and chew the forest. A tongue or tongues often mention it. Being yoked to a pole to waft the offering to the gods, he is often compared to or directly called a steed. Often, he is compared to a bird, winged and darting in rapid flight to the gods.

While his luster resembles the rays of Dawn and the lightning flashes of a raincloud, his track, his fellies, and the furrows made by his steeds are black.

The wind drives him through the woods. The barber with a beard invades the forests and shaves the earth's hairs. The roar of his flames is like the roar of the sea. When his grass-devouring sparks arise, he bellows like a bull when he invades the forest trees. In the manner of the erector of a pillar, he supports the sky with his smoke; one of his distinctive epithets is "smoke-bannered." He is drawn by two or more ruddy or tawny horses and driven by the wind. He yokes them to invoke the gods, for he is the charioteer of the offering.

God is born living. Poetry dwells on the poet's births, forms, and abodes. By friction between the two firesticks, Agni is generated every day. His parents produced him as an infant with a hard time catching him. Children devour their parents as soon as they are born. It is said that the ten maidens who produced him are the ten fingers used in twirling the good fire drill. To kindle a flame, Agni must create powerful friction. Because the fire is lit every morning for the offering, Agni is described as "waking at dawn." Hence, he is the "youngest" of the gods; however, he is also old since he conducted the first offering. Thus, he comes to be simultaneously called both "ancient" and "very young" in the same passage.

In addition to springing from the air, Agni is often said to have come from Heaven. The triple nature of Agni is often attributed to his birth on earth and in Heaven. He was made threefold by the gods. There are three births in his life, and he has three places of abode or dwelling. This earliest Indian Trinity is essential as the basis of much of the mystical speculation of the Vedic period. From Heaven first Agni was born, from us (men) a second time, and from water a third time. There is no suspicion that this is the prototype of the later Rigvedic triad, Sun, Wind, Fire, which is spoken of as distributed in the three worlds, as well as the classic trio, Sun, Indra, Fire, though not Rigvedic.

Brahma, Vishnu, and Civa may also be the historical progenitors of this Trinity. According to the Brahmana cult, the division of a single sacrificial fire into three may have been suggested by this triad of fires.

Agni, who abides in every family, house, and dwelling, is also said to have many births due to the multiplicity of terrestrial fires. The one he is, strewn in many places, is but one. The king is the same. He is connected to other fires, like the branches of a tree. All the gods he surrounds as a felly the spokes are embodied in him in various forms and names. As a result, the speculations about Agni's various forms lead to the monotheistic notion of unity pervading the many manifestations of the divine. Despite being immortal, Agni has taken up residence among mortals; he is constantly referred to as a "guest" in human homes, and he is the only God to be addressed as g*ihapati, "lord of the house."

Agni is repeatedly described as a "messenger" who moves between Heaven and Earth and as a priest who conducts offerings. As Indra is the noble warrior, he is the great priest.

Additionally, Agni is an influential benefactor of his devotees. With a thousand eyes, he watches over his worshippers' oblations but consumes their enemies like dry bushes and destroys them like a tree struck by lightning. He issues all blessings as branches of a tree. All prizes are collected in him, and he opens the door to wealth. As Spring in the desert, he gives rain from Heaven. Indra, however, grants mainly victories, booty, power, and glory, while he grants domestic welfare, offspring, and general prosperity.

As the soma offering is an integral part of the Rigveda ritual, God Soma is naturally one of its principal deities. Only a few hymns are scattered throughout the ninth book. As a result, Soma ranks third among the Vedic gods based on the frequency of mention. The presence of the soma plant and its juice before their eyes limits the imagination of the poets who describe its personification.

Nine books of incantations are sung over the Soma as it is pressed by stones and flowed through a woolen strainer into wooden vats, where it is offered as a beverage to the gods. Poets chiefly involve these processes, overlaying them with chaotic depictions and mystical fantasies. Soma is purified by the ten maidens who are sisters or by the daughters of Vivasvat (the rising Sun). The human form and actions of Soma are thus little discussed. He was chewed on by a cow's hide as the stones pounded the shoots on a skin.

After passing through a sheep's wool filter, juice flows into jars or vats. Like buffaloes, soma streams rush towards the forests of vats. The gods fly into the vats like birds. Tawny One drops like a bird sitting on a branch in the bowls. Like a roaring bull on the herd, Soma is said to rush into the water's lap when mixed with water in the vat. Running around the vat, he is impelled by the singers. The ten maidens cleanse him in the wood while he plays.

The Rigvedic period is characterized by an evolution of thought from concrete to abstract. This tendency results in the creation of abstract deities, which are rare, mainly in the last book. One short hymn invokes Faith, while two others invoke Wrath, such as Craddha, "Faith." In later Vedas, these abstractions become more frequent. The

Kama, "Desire," first appears in the Atharva-Veda, where he is mentioned with arrows piercing hearts; he is the precursor of the flower-arrowed God of love.

It is also possible to find deities whose names indicate an agent, such as Dhatri, "Creator," or an aspect, such as Prajapati, "Lord of Creatures," among the abstractions. Rather than appearing to be direct abstractions, these seem to be derived from epithets that initially applied to one or older deities but later became independent from them. In a later verse of the last book, Prajapati, originally a nickname for gods like Savitri and Soma, appears as a distinct deity. This God is in the Atharva-Veda and the Vajasaneyi-Samhita.

Recognized as the chief deity by the Brahmanas regularly. The Sutras identify Prajapati with Brahma, his successor in the post-Vedic era.

A refrain appears here after nine successive stanzas, in which the Creator is referred to as unknown, with the interrogative pronoun ka, "what?" Later in Vedic literature, this kain became the epithet of the Creator Prajapati and even an independent name.

Brihaspati, Lord of Prayer," is a deity of an abstract character found in the oldest and the latest parts of the Rigveda. Roth and other renowned Vedic scholars regard him as a direct representation of devotion. Although he has much in common with Agni, the present writer considers him only an indirect deification of his sacrificial activity. Therefore, his priesthood is his most prominent characteristic. His roots are firmly rooted in the myths of Indra, much like Agni's. He often drove out the cows after defeating Vala, the demon. As the divine Brahma priest, Brihaspati may have been Brahma's prototype, the Hindu trinity chief. The name Brihaspati survived in post-Vedic mythology as the title of a sage, the teacher of the gods, and the ruler of the planet Jupiter.

The goddess Aditi is another abstraction of a peculiar kind. Even though she is not the subject of any separate hymn, she is frequently celebrated incidentally.

Only two characteristics stand out about her. First, she is the mother of the Adityas, whose chief is Varuna. Secondly, like her son Varuna, she can free herself from physical suffering and moral guilt. This trait is reflected in her name, which means "unbinding" or "freedom."

There are a few passages in the Rigveda that retain the unpersonified sense. The origin of the abstraction can probably be explained as follows: a poet prays for the "secure and unlimited gift of Aditi." When first used, the term "sons of Aditi" probably meant "sons of liberation" to emphasize a salient trait characteristic of the Rigveda. In Sanskrit, the feminine word "liberation" (Aditi) would have been personified by a process with over one parallel. Aditi, a goddess of Indian origin, is considerably younger than some of her sons, dating back to pre-Indian times.

In Vedic belief, goddesses hold a very subordinate position. The world is hardly ruled by them. Ushas is the only one of any significance. Among the male gods, Sarasvati ranks only the least prominent. Apart from Prithivi, Ratri, Night is one of the few to whom an entire hymn is dedicated. As with her sister Dawn, with whom she is often paired, she is managed as a daughter of the sky. She is envisioned not as the dark but as the bright starlit Night. Thus, in comparing the twin goddesses, a poet says, "One decks herself with stars, with sunlight the other."

Vedic mythology is unique in invoking several deities whose names are combined as dual compounds. A dozen of these pairs are celebrated in entire hymns and another half-dozen in separate stanzas. In this way, the most often found names are Heaven and Earth (Dyavaprithivi), which are most often combined with Mitra-Varuna. This favorite formation can be ascribed to the last couple without a doubt. The myth of their marriage has been widely disseminated among primitive peoples since their association dates back to the Indo-European period.

The gods are not the only deities associated with definite groups of divine beings. As we have seen, the Maruts are the largest and most important of these gods, who constantly attend Indra on his warlike exploits. They are sometimes associated with their father, Rudra, under Rudras. Their mother, Aditi, or their chief Varuna are frequently mentioned in association with the smaller Aditya group. The number is given as seven or eight in two passages of the Rigveda, but in the Brahmanas and later, it is usually twelve. About eight or ten hymns are collectively addressed to them in the Rigveda.

A third and much less critical group is the Vasus, primarily associated with Indra in the Rigveda but led by Agni in later Vedic texts. There are no individual names or substantial numbers related to this group. Eight of them, however, are mentioned in the Brahmanas. Lastly, some sixty hymns are dedicated to the Vicvedevas or All-gods. Factitious sacrificial groups are meant to encompass the entire pantheon, so no one should be excluded from invocations addressed to everyone. Interestingly, the All-gods is sometimes seen as a smaller group, invoked alongside the Vasus and Aditya.

Besides the higher gods, the Rigveda mentions several mythical beings not regarded as possessing the divine nature from the beginning. In eleven hymns, the Ribhus form a triad and are addressed. Due to their exceptional skill, they have often been considered deities due to their deft hands. The most remarkable feat of dexterity by which they became gods—in which they appear as successful rivals of the artificer god Tvashtri—was to transform his bowl into four shining cups.

---

THE FOUR CUPS OF THIS bowl represent the phases of the moon. The Ribhus are also said to have refreshed their parents' youth, by whom Heaven and Earth were meant to be divided. This miraculous act seems to be directly related to another myth about them. They slept for twelve days in the house of the Sun, Agohya ("who cannot be disguised"). The Ribhus likely stayed at the Sun's place during the winter solstice, when the lunar year of 354 was intercalated with the solar year of 366 days and the days got longer.

According to the various myths illustrative of remarkable skill, the Ribhus were probably originally terrestrial or a*rial elves, whose dexterity gradually attracted legends describing their impressive skills. Several passages of the Rigveda mention a celestial water-nymph called Apsaras ("moving in the waters") as the spouse of a male genius named Gandharva. Occasionally, more than one Apsarase is mentioned. Apsaras smile at her beloved in Heaven, according to the poet. Their abode is in the later Vedas, where their lutes and cymbals resound throughout trees.

Gandharvas and men alike love the Apsaras. Brahmanas describe them as beautiful and devoted to dancing, singing, and playing. They become the courtesans of Indra's Heaven after the Vedic period. Urvaci was one such individual. In a relatively obscure hymn of the Rigveda, she speaks with her earthly husband, Pururavas.

A more detailed and connected version of the story can be found in the Catapatha Brahmana. There is a condition attached to the alliance between Urvaci and Pururavas. As soon as the Gandharvas break this stratagem, the nymph vanishes from her lover's sight. Despite his refusal, her lover receives immortality's promise (like Tithonus) for returning. While wandering searching for her, Pururavas spots her swimming in a lotus lake as an aquatic bird with other Apsarases. As a result of his entreaties, Urvaci agrees to return once after a year after discovering herself to him. Kalidasa's play Vikramorvaci was based on this myth in the post-Vedic era.

It appears that Gandharva was initially conceived as a single entity. In the Rigveda, the name almost always appears in the singular, and in the Avesta, where it occurs a few times as Gandarewa, it seems only in the singular. Additionally, he guards the celestial Soma and is sometimes associated with water, as in the Avesta. There is a stereotyped association between the Gandharvas and the Apsarases in the later Vedas. During the post-Vedic era, they became celestial singers, and one of their Sanskrit names was "City of the Gandharvas.". It means "miracle."

One of the most important ancient priests and heroes in Rigveda is Manu, humanity's first offering and ancestor. The sages refer to him as "our father" and speak of offerings as "the people of Manu." The Catapatha Brahmana makes Manu play the part of a Noah in the history of human descent.

In the capture's myth of the cows, the Angirases are strongly associated with Indra. A second ancient race of mythical priests is the Bhrigus, to whom Mataricvan, the Indian Prometheus, brought the hidden Agni from Heaven, which established and diffused the sacrificial fire on earth.

Rigveda rarely mentions the seven rishis as an ancestor priestly group. According to the Brahmanas, they are the seven stars in the Great Bear constellation and were created at the beginning of time. This curious identification was doubtless brought about partly by the sameness of the number in the two cases and partly by the similarity of sound between Rishi, "seer," and riksha, which in the Rigveda means both "star" and "bear."

———⊚———

THE VEDAS PLACE A GREAT deal of emphasis on animals in their mythological and religious conceptions. The horse has several names, including drawing the gods' cars and representing the Sun. Fire and the Sun were defined by the horse in Vedic rituals. Horse offering was practiced in Indian antiquity according to two hymns in the Rigveda that deal with the subject.

The cow, however, appears most frequently in Rigveda. Even in remote periods of Indian history, this animal occupied a critical position due to its preeminent utility. A cow is a beam of Dawn, and a cloud is a cloud. Under the personification of Pricni, "the speckled one," the rain cloud is a cow, the mother of the Storm-gods. The abundant clouds on which all wealth in India rested were doubtless the prototypes of the many-colored cows that yield all desires in the Heaven of the blest described by the Atharva-Veda and forerunners of the "Cow of Plenty" (Kamaduh) so familiar to post-Vedic poetry.

Earth is often referred to as a cow in Rigveda. The cow was already considered sacred because Rishi addressed her as Aditi and a goddess, urging her not to be killed. According to the Rigveda, the cow is often designated as Aghnya ("not divine"). Avesta evidence indicates that the sanctity of this animal dates back to Indo-Iranian times. Cow worship is fully recognized in the Atharva-Veda, while beef consumption is condemned in the Atapatha Brahmana.

Cow sanctity has survived in India down to the present day and has even grown stronger over the years. During the Indian Mutiny, greased cartridges played an important role. No other animal has owed humankind so much, and in India, the debt has been repaid with a level of veneration unmatched elsewhere. The cow has proven to be such a significant factor in Indian life, and thought that an in-depth account of her influence from the beginning would form an essential part of the history of civilization.

One of the most prominent noxious animals in the Rigveda is the serpent. According to legend, this is the form of the powerful demon, the foe of Indra. As Ahi buddha, "the Dragon of the Deep," the snake appears as a divine being in the aerial ocean's fathomless depths and represents the character's beneficent side, Vritra. As well as the Gandharvas and others, snakes are mentioned as semi-divine beings in the later Vedas, and Sutras prescribe offerings to them.

Throughout the latter works, we meet the Nagas serpents and humans only in form for the first time. In post-Vedic times, serpent worship was widespread throughout India. Since it is not mentioned in the Rigveda but is widespread among non-Aryan Indians, it seems likely that when the Aryans reached India, the land of serpents, they found the cult diffused among the aborigines and borrowed it.

Plants are frequently invoked as divinities, especially in enumerations of waters, rivers, mountains, Heaven, and earth. The sole aim of one hymn is to praise plants (shade) for their healing properties. A large tree is adored, and plants are offered during wedding processions in later Vedic texts. Aranyani, the mocking genius of the woods, is personified in one hymn of the Rigveda. The weird sights and sounds of the night are here captured with a delicate perception of nature in the dark emptiness of the jungle.

When viewed as beneficial to man, objects crafted by man's hand are occasionally deified and worshipped as religious objects pointing back to remote antiquity. The primary purpose of these implements is sacrificial. In the tenth book, three psalms commemorate the pressing stones used in preparing Soma, while one hymn invokes the sacrificial post (called "lord of the forest"). A few stanzas encapsulate the plot; one hymn praises various war implements, while another in the Atharva-Veda praises the drum.

There are two classes of demons described in the Rigveda. One consists of the gods' aerial adversaries.

As per the older view, there is a conflict between a single god and a single demon. The gods and the demons were then seen as opposing hosts arrayed against each other. Brahmanas frequently portray antagonism in this way. There is a familiar name for the gods' aerial foes: Asura. There is a remarkable history behind this word. The Rigveda refers to the gods, while the Avesta refers to Ahura, the highest God of Zoroastrianism. When used by itself in the later parts of the Rigveda, asura also signifies "deity," which is its only meaning in the

Atharva-Veda. A somewhat unsuccessful attempt has been made to explain how a word signifying "god" came to mean "technology" as a result of national conflicts, in which the Asuras or gods of extra-Vedic tribes became demons to the Vedic Indians, just as the devas or gods of the Veda are to the Avesta.

There is no solid argument to back up this view, which is opposed by the fact that for the Rigvedic Indian, asura was not just an image of a divine being but was particularly associated with Varuṇa, the most exalted of the gods. The Veda itself must have changed its meaning of the word over time. There is a sense of "possession of power" here, which could potentially apply to hostile entities. As a consequence, both reasons appear in a Rigvedic hymn. As the Rigvedic period progressed, the word's application to the gods diminished. Due to a need for a word denoting hostile demoniac powers and an incipient popular etymology, which saw a negative (a-sura) in the world, the sura, "god," was created in the Upanishads.

# BIBLIOGRAPHY

The Rigveda: The Earliest Religious Poetry of India. Vol. 1–3. Translated by Stephanie W. Jamison; Joel P. Brereton.

Stephanie W. Jamison (tr.); Joel P. Brereton (tr.) (2014). The Rigveda: The Earliest Religious Poetry of India. 3-volume set.

Stephanie W. Jamison (tr.); Joel P. Brereton (tr.) (2014a). The Rigveda: The Earliest Religious Poetry of India. Vol. 1.

editio princeps: Friedrich Max Müller, The Hymns of the Rigveda, with Sayana's commentary, London.

Theodor Aufrecht, 2nd ed., Bonn, 1877.

Sontakke, N. S. (1933). Rgveda-Samhitā: Śrimat-Sāyanāchārya virachita-bhāṣya-sametā. Sāyanachārya (commentary) (First ed.). Vaidika Samśodhana Maṇḍala.. The editorial board for the First Edition included N. S. Sontakke (Managing Editor), V. K. Rājvade, M. M. Vāsudevaśāstri, and T. S. Varadarājaśarmā.

B. van Nooten und G. Holland, Rig Veda, a metrically restored text, Department of Sanskrit and Indian Studies.

Rgveda-Samhita, Text in Devanagari, English translation Notes and indices by H. H. Wilson, Ed. W. F. Webster, originally in 1888, Published Nag Publishers 1990, 11A/U.A. Jawaharnagar, Delhi-7.

Sri Aurobindo (1998), The Secret of veda .

Sri Aurobindo, Hymns to the Mystic Fire (Commentary on the Rig Veda).

Raimundo Pannikar (1972), The Vedic Experience.

Harold G. Coward (1990). The Philosophy of the Grammarians, in Encyclopedia of Indian Philosophies Volume 5 (Editor: Karl Potter).

Vashishtha Narayan Jha, A Linguistic Analysis of the Rgveda-Padapatha Sri Satguru Publications, Delhi (1992).

Bjorn Merker, Rig Veda Riddles In Nomad Perspective, 1988.

Oberlies, Thomas (1998).

Oldenberg, Hermann (1894). Hymnen des Rigveda. 1. Teil: Metrische und textgeschichtliche Prolegomena. Berlin 1888. (please add), Wiesbaden 1982.

Adolf Kaegi, The Rigveda: The Oldest Literature of the Indians, Boston.(1886)

Mallory, J. P.; et al. (1989). Indo-Iranian Languages in Encyclopedia of Indo-European Culture.

Anthony, David W. (2007), The Horse The Wheel And Language. How Bronze-Age Riders From the Eurasian Steppes Shaped The Modern World,

Avari, Burjor (2007), India: The Ancient Past.

Bryant, Edwin (2001). The Quest for the Origins of Vedic Culture: The Indo-Aryan Migration Debate.

Dwyer, Rachel (2013), What Do Hindus Believe?,

Flood, Gavin D. (1996), An Introduction to Hinduism.

George Erdosy (1995). The Indo-Aryans of Ancient South Asia.

Hexam, Irving (2011), Understanding World Religions: An Interdisciplinary Approach.

Gregory Possehl; Michael Witzel (2002). "Vedic". In Peter N. Peregrine; Melvin Ember (eds.).

Lal, B.B. 2005. The Homeland of the Aryans. Evidence of Rigvedic Flora and Fauna & Archaeology.

Talageri, Shrikant: The Rigveda:

Witzel, Michael (1995), "Early Sanskritization: Origin and Development of the Kuru state".

Witzel, Michael (1997), "The Development of the Vedic Canon and its Schools: The Social and Political Milieu".

Witzel, Michael (2003). "Vedas and Upanisads". In Flood, Gavin (ed.). The Blackwell Companion to Hinduism.

Witzel, Michael (2019). "Beyond the Flight of the Falcon". In Thapar, Romila (ed.). Which of Us are Aryans?.

Wood, Michael (2007), The Story of India Hardcover.

Antonova, K.A.; Bongard-Levin, G.; Kotovsky, G. (1979). [History of India]

Asher, C.B.; Talbot, C (1 January 2008), India Before Europe (1st ed.),

Bandyopadhyay, Sekhar (2004), From Plassey to Partition: A History of Modern India

Bayly, Christopher Alan (2000) [1996], Empire and Information: Intelligence Gathering and Social Communication in India, 1780–1870

Bose, Sugata; Jalal, Ayesha (2003), Modern South Asia: History, Culture, Political Economy (2nd ed.)

Brown, Judith M. (1994), Modern India: The Origins of an Asian Democracy (2nd ed.)

Bentley, Jerry H. (June 1996), "Cross-Cultural Interaction and Periodization in World History"

Daniélou, Alain (2003), A Brief History of India, Rochester

Datt, Ruddar; Sundharam, K.P.M. (2009), Indian Economy

Devi, Ragini (1990). Dance Dialects of India.

Doniger, Wendy, ed. (1999). Merriam-Webster's Encyclopedia of World Religions.

Eaton, Richard M. (2005), A Social History of the Deccan: 1300–1761: Eight Indian Lives

Fay, Peter Ward (1993), The forgotten army : India's armed struggle for independence

Kamath, Suryanath U. (2001) [1980], A concise history of Karnataka

Keay, John (2000), India: A History

Kenoyer, J. Mark (1998). The Ancient Cities of the Indus Valley Civilisation.

Kulke, Hermann; Rothermund, Dietmar (2004) [First published 1986], A History of India (4th ed.),

Law, R. C. C. (1978), "North Africa in the Hellenistic and Roman periods, 323 BC to AD 305", in Fage, J.D.; Oliver, Roland (eds.)

Ludden, D. (2002), India and South Asia: A Short History, One World

Meri, Josef W. (2005), Medieval Islamic Civilization: An Encyclopedia

Michaels, Axel (2004), Hinduism. Past and present

Niyogi, Roma (1959). The History of the Gāhaḍavāla Dynasty

Petraglia, Michael D.; Allchin, Bridget (2007). The Evolution and History of Human Populations in South Asia: Inter-disciplinary Studies in Archaeology, Biological Anthropology

Reddy, Krishna (2003). Indian History. New Delhi

Sastri, K. A. Nilakanta (1955). A history of South India from prehistoric times to the fall of Vijayanagar.

Schomer, Karine; McLeod, W.H., eds. (1987). The Sants: Studies in a Devotional Tradition of India.

Sen, Sailendra Nath (1 January 1999). Ancient Indian History and Civilization.

Singh, Upinder (2008), A History of Ancient and Early Medieval India: From the Stone Age to the 12th Century

Sircar, D C (1990), "Pragjyotisha-Kamarupa", in Barpujari, H K (ed.), The Comprehensive History of Assam, vol. I

Thapar, Romila (1977), A History of India. Volume One

# APPENDIX
# PHOTO COLLAGE

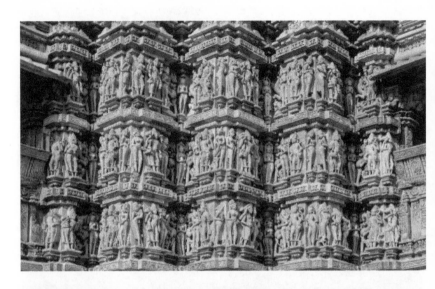

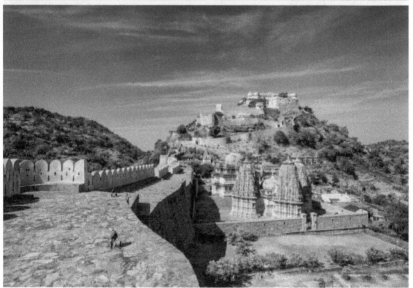

# Don't miss out!

Visit the website below and you can sign up to receive emails whenever HENRY ROMANO publishes a new book. There's no charge and no obligation.

https://books2read.com/r/B-A-VFVN-PFOAC

**BOOKS 2 READ**

Connecting independent readers to independent writers.

Did you love *Mysteries of the Rig Veda*? Then you should read *Ancient India and the Vedic Gods*[1] by HENRY ROMANO!

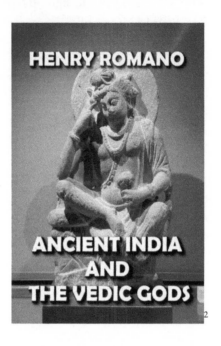

These four Vedas comprise a highly developed religious system - the Rig, Sama, Atharva, and Yajur Vedas. Through the worship of the demigods, or the Vedic gods, these Vedas were primarily intended to encourage the satisfaction of material desires. Thus, the Vedas clearly explain how to perform the required worship and sacrifices or rituals to these devas (demigods) to receive the blessings required to increase one's power and position or reach the heavens in the future or for other purposes.

The point is that the devas participate and affect all universal management and activities, including the weather or who is blessed with certain opulence, such as riches, beautiful spouses, large families,

1. https://books2read.com/u/b5lDZO

2. https://books2read.com/u/b5lDZO

good health, etc. A person could worship Agni to gain power, Durgadevi to obtain good fortune, Indra to have a healthy sexual life, or Vasus to earn money. Karma-kanda is the section of the Vedas that many consider the most essential part of Vedic teachings. Thus, people will be able to live a good life and enjoy a decent existence. Of course, various actions, or karmas, are motivated by our aspirations to achieve specific results. Several sections in the Vedas deal with Karma-Kanda. Although this is not the complete understanding of the karma-kanda segment, which provides rituals for purifying our minds and actions in pursuit of our desires, and not limiting ourselves to only acquiring everything that one needs from the demigods. One's habits and thoughts become purified when one has faith and steadiness in the performance of the ritual. As one becomes pure and free of those desires, one gradually acquires one's needs and assuages one's desires. When we purify our consciousness, we can achieve a higher level of spiritual activity. The karma-kanda rituals had this higher purpose. Unless one recognizes this, one misses the point and remains attached to ways to satisfy material desires, which will keep one in earthly existence.

Read more at https://www.dttvpublications.com/henryromano.

# Also by HENRY ROMANO

Myths and Legends of Japan
Myths and Legends of the Norse
The Ancient Mythologies of Peru and Mexico
Vedic Cosmology
Hindu Mythology and the Origins of Gods
Vedic Cosmos
Vedic Philosophy of the Kali Yuga
Sanskrit Mysteries of Vedic India
Ancient India and the Vedic Gods
The Secrets of Brahma
A History of Lost Knowledge in Sanskrit Literature
The Rise of Civilizations Concerning Vedic Knowledge
Decoding Hindu Chronology
Mysteries of the Rig Veda

Watch for more at https://www.dttvpublications.com/henryromano.

# About the Author

Henry Romano, also known in India as Manu Radhesh, was educated in Hertfordshire, in England, formally trained as a British archaeologist, who subsequently excavated the numerous ruins of the ancient cities of the Indus Valley. He has uncovered evidence of sophisticated civilizations. which he he refers to as 'Vedic Civilization One'. His work on Vedic Cosmology was one of archaeology's major achievements and greatly advanced the study of Indian, Vedic, Sumerian and indeed World prehistory. He is currently working on the Ancient Origins of Latin America.

Read more at https://www.dttvpublications.com/henryromano.

# About the Publisher

During this ever-changing publishing industry, DTTV Publications (formerly DTTV Studios Broadcast Press) has been at the forefront. For over 30+ years, we have been successfully publishing high quality books with the experience and integrity that a great publisher demands. In 33 countries around the world, we've published over 2,000 titles. In addition to working with charities, we support causes that are important to us and our authors. Our imprints include fiction, non-fiction, children's, educational, and poetry titles. See below for more information. The authors we work with can opt for either traditional or hybrid contracts. By doing so, we provide a level playing field for both established and new authors. We have dedicated departments that are solely dedicated to our authors. Their knowledge and expertise will ensure your work is taken care of from production through to marketing to the highest standard possible. We are able to fill orders quickly around the world because we have our own warehouse and distribution center. As part of our ethical policy, we monitor our production and office practices to minimize harmful effects on the natural world environment. Please read our submission guidelines if you are interested in submitting your work to us.